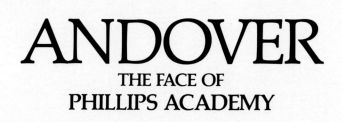

ANDOVER
THE FACE OF
PHILLIPS ACADEMY

*. . . to learn The GREAT END
and REAL BUSINESS of Living.*

Samuel Phillips, Jr.
The Constitution of Phillips Academy

A Focus Book

Published by
The Ipswich Press
Ipswich, Massachusetts 01938

ISBN Number 0-938864-07-6

Printed in Japan by Dai Nippon

ANDOVER

THE FACE OF PHILLIPS ACADEMY

Photography and Text by Mia Kelly
Foreword by Thomas H. Wyman

DEDICATION

Phillips Academy, Andover,
exists, above all,
in the minds and hearts
of those who have been here.

But Andover Hill is also a place
of singular physical beauty
in architecture and landscape.

I hope that these photographs
may capture some of that beauty,
and perhaps recall some of that spirit,
and I respectfully dedicate this volume
to that great company
of which I am proud to be a part,
the students and teachers,
past and present,
of Phillips Academy, Andover.

Mia Kelly, P.A. 1983

The Great Seal was "cut" by Paul Revere in 1782. The Latin inscriptions reflect the founder's belief in the importance of secondary education, *FINIS ORIGINE PENDET:* (The End Depends on the Beginning); and his conviction that the benefits of a superior education must be used for the good of others, *NON SIBI:* (Not for One's Self).

FOREWORD

It has been suggested that as our world moves with increasing complexity and speed we should pause more frequently to recognize the beautiful, to celebrate the worthy and to savour a sense of history and tradition. We should not be too self-conscious about acknowledging small love affairs with places where we have spent time which has been important to us.

For many this book will offer one of these opportunities. Photographed and written by a young woman who saw and cared, it will provide a reminder for many — and a first look for others — of a remarkably beautiful setting where important things have been going on for over 200 years of American history. Somehow it seems appropriate that this has been a place for the pursuit of excellence and the development of leaders.

For those who are involved with Phillips Academy it is a matter of special pride that Mia Kelly took these pictures and prepared this text while she was an undergraduate at the school. I am grateful to an old friend for taking us on such a good walk.

Thomas H. Wyman, P.A. 1947
Trustee, Phillips Academy
Chairman and Chief Executive
CBS, Inc.

George Washington visited the school and sent his nephews here.

"The End depends upon the Beginning"
Motto of Phillips Academy

The Beginning was thirteen students meeting for the first time in a single room on April 21, 1778.

Samuel Phillips, Jr., was then twenty six years old. The United States had not yet been formed. The outcome of the American Revolution was in grave doubt. George Washington's army had retreated to Valley Forge, enduring the "Days that Try Men's Souls".

But Samuel Phillips believed that the Revolution would succeed and, much as he supported the American Cause, he also recognized that the loss of British tradition and authority would leave a major gap in American life. The challenges of the future would require better educated leaders.

He wrote: "Upon the sound education of children depends the comfort or grief of parents, the welfare or disorder of the community, the glory or ruin of the state".

*   *   *

Phillips Academy today is an impressive academic community of over 1200 students, with an extensive faculty offering 290 courses. It occupies a magnificent hilltop campus of 500 acres, with more than 160 buildings and facilities of every kind, in the middle of Andover, about one-half hour north of Boston.

Despite the dramatic physical changes, the founder's original principles still guide the school: a rigorous moral and intellectual training for leadership; a concept of service, *Non Sibi*, not for one's self; a dedication to the "great end and real business of living;" for "youth from every quarter."

Samuel Phillips Hall.

The Phillips family dates from the earliest days of Massachusetts Bay Colony and their influence courses through the history of American education. The first was George Phillips, a 1613 graduate of Cambridge University, who left England with Governor John Winthrop in 1630 as the first company clergyman. Education, especially theological education, was of great concern to these staunch Pilgrims. The Puritan faith was in disfavor in the England of Charles I and the doors of Oxford and Cambridge were closed to the colonist's sons. The solution was a university of their own, founded in 1636 in the village of Cambridge on the Charles River and named for a young clergyman, John Harvard, who had left his library of 400 books to the school.

The Phillips sons were all educated at Harvard and the eldest in each generation was named Samuel (to the confusion of later historians). By the 1750's, the fourth generation had produced the parson of Andover, grandfather of Samuel Phillips, Jr. Some sense of the man and the times may be gained from his response, when asked if he was the parson who served there, replied, "I am, sir, the parson who rules here!"

For all their piety, the parson's sons also turned their minds to business and began to amass considerable fortunes. Samuel Phillips, Sr., son of the parson, prospered in Andover, investing in a variety of ventures, most notably, if not most profitably, the construction of a gunpowder mill on the Shawsheen River to supply powder when George Washington's army was besieged in Boston. John Phillips, uncle of the Founder, moved to Exeter, New Hampshire, traded in timber for masts for the Royal Navy, speculated in land, became a leading banker — and developed an interest in education.

Although a Harvard graduate like his family before him, he became a trustee of Dartmouth, newly founded in New Hampshire by a Yale man, and also contributed substantially to the College of New Jersey, which had moved from Newark to start over at Princeton in 1757. Both the senior Phillipses shared an interest in a new school at Andover — and so Samuel Phillips dream of Phillips Academy came into being in April 1778.

Pearson Hall, the home of the Classics Department, is named for the first Headmaster Eliphalet Pearson. The stern visage seems appropriate.

By 1781, encouraged by what had been accomplished in the three years of existence of Phillips Academy at Andover, John Phillips founded Phillips Exeter Academy. At his death, John Phillips divided his estate among the two Phillips' Academies, Dartmouth and Princeton, leaving nothing to his alma mater, Harvard, which he had come to suspect of liberal leanings.

The Puritan faith required constant vigilance. Samuel Phillips' father had written him at Harvard in 1771 to guard against the unwholesome influences of the city; "Don't go to Boston and beware of all that comes from Boston." Nevertheless, Samuel Phillips, Jr. married a Boston girl, Phoebe Foxcroft. In 1775, as the guns of Revolution fired at Bunker Hill, Phillips was charged with moving the books from the Harvard Library to Andover for safekeeping.

Phillips was joined in Andover by his Harvard classmate and friend, Eliphalet Pearson, a brilliant scholar with fervent religious convictions. Pearson had married the daughter of President Holyoke of Harvard, taught at the local grammar school in Andover and assisted the Phillips at the powder mill. As Samuel Phillips' dream took form, it was logical that Pearson should become the first headmaster. He served until 1786, when he returned to Harvard as Professor of Hebrew and Oriental Languages. Nevertheless, he continued to exert a dominating influence on the school as a member of the board over the next forty years, serving as President following the death of Samuel Phillips in 1802. When the Harvard faculty voted to turn Unitarian, Pearson returned in outrage to Andover in 1808 to found the Andover Theological Seminary, which shared Andover Hill and functioned as the center of New England Puritanism through the nineteenth century, until it was finally absorbed into Phillips Academy.

Pearson was succeeded as headmaster by Ebenezer Pemberton, a professor at Princeton, where he had as pupils both James Madison and Aaron Burr. But this, and later changes in headmasters, had little effect on the school. The guiding principles laid down by Samuel Phillips served as a constant compass for the direction of the school. Pearson's standards of stern discipline and concentration on the classics lasted until the arrival of Cecil Bancroft a century later.

Front door — Bulfinch Hall.

Overleaf: The Headmasters House was built in 1811 as part of the Andover Theological Seminary. In its over 205 years of existence, Phillips Academy has had only twelve headmasters since Eliphalet Pearson. The present Headmaster is Donald McNemar, who was formerly Associate Dean of Faculty at Dartmouth. Mr. McNemar took office in 1982, succeeding Theodore Sizer, who had come to Andover in 1972 from the Deanship of the School of Education at Harvard.

Designed by Charles Bulfinch, the most famous early American architect, and built in 1818, as a gift from William Phillips of Boston, Bulfinch Hall has been a gymnasium and a dining hall. It was restored in 1930 through a gift from Edward S. Harkness of Standard Oil who also donated the residential colleges to Yale, the "Houses" to Harvard, as well as major gifts to Exeter. Today it is the home of the English department.

Pearson Hall, originally built as the chapel of the Andover Theological Seminary, is named for the first Headmaster.

Stuart House was built in 1812 for Moses Stuart, Professor of Sacred Literature at Andover Theological Seminary. In addition to his teaching, Stuart ran the Andover Theological Press, which became under his guidance the only press in America capable of printing Greek and Hebrew. Eleven Oriental languages were added and Andover became a center for exotic languages and missionary publications. Today Stuart House is the residence of Joseph Mesics, Secretary of Phillips Academy.

Stowe House was built in 1828 as a carpenters shop for the Theological
Seminary on the site of the present Andover Inn. During the 1850's it was the
residence of Professor Calvin E. Stowe, whose wife, Harriet Beecher Stowe,
wrote *Uncle Tom's Cabin*. Today it is a faculty residence.

Samaritan House was built in 1824, on the site where Cochran Chapel now stands. It was used as a residence by several headmasters before being moved across the road as part of Cochran's redevelopment of the campus. Samaritan House is now a master's residence and a dormitory.

Overleaf: The towers of modern Phillips Academy rise above the tree line.

The Memorial Bell Tower stands on the field where Andover men trained for the Revolutionary War and were later addressed by George Washington. It was designed by Guy Lowell as a gift from the Fuller family to commemorate the eighty-nine graduates who fell in World War I.

Detail of Bulfinch tower.

Samuel Phillips Hall Tower.

Borden Gym tower.

Detail of Memorial tower.

Entrance to the Elm Arch fronting the East Quadrangle.

The Admissions Office is generally the first contact with the school for every new student. Director of Admissions is Josh Miner, a charming, tweedy, bow-tied gentleman of the old school, who also is a founder and former president of Outward Bound. A red convertible parked outside signifies his presence.

Cochran Chapel is the only building named after Thomas Cochran, the single individual most responsible for the physical structure and appearance of modern Andover.

Cochran, much in line with Samuel Phillips' thinking, believed deeply in the importance of secondary education and he felt that relatively too much attention was paid to universities. As he put it, "every thoughtful man admits character transcends intellect. . . at preparatory school. . . character is in a more formative state than in university life later on." His contributions to Andover were intended to permit it to serve as an example to other secondary schools.

Born in St. Paul, Minnesota, a member of the class of 1890, Cochran followed a strong Andover tradition to Yale — at its high point in 1936 ninety Andover graduates, more than half of the class, went to Yale, where they accounted for more than 10% of the Yale freshman class.

Cochran later became a partner of J.P. Morgan and amassed a large fortune, virtually all of which he devoted to the Andover campus, completely restructuring the "Great Quadrangle," including Samuel Phillips Hall dominating the East, George Washington the North, Samuel F.B. Morse (P.A. 1865) the South, with the Addision Gallery and the Oliver Wendell Holmes (P.A. 1825) Library anchoring the North and South wings of the entrance. His "Grand Design" also required removal of several existing buildings to new locations and the opening of a "Vista" to the West and the residential area of the "West Quad."

He was a strong-willed man and his work at the school was not without frustrations. One piece of correspondence bears his handwritten comment, "Kill the architect!" Cochran was also not inflexible; he recognized that change might be necessary and so he provided that his trustess could modify the conditions of his gifts by a three-fourths vote, plus the subsequent approval of the Chief Justice of the Massachusetts Supreme Judicial Court and the Presidents of Yale and Harvard.

During his building program he sought to avoid publicity and would never permit any of his buildings to bear his name. However, with the completion of the chapel, balancing the Memorial Bell Tower across the open lawn, he felt his work was complete, and he finally consented to the use of his name.

Oliver Wendell Holmes graduated in the class of 1825.

Spring brings bright colors everywhere — even professors' trousers.

The grim influence of Calvinistic thought had hung heavy over the school in its early days. Of all the Arts, music alone, and sacred music at that, was all that seemed proper. Thomas Cochran believed that lives of students would be enriched from the presence of great art and, in keeping with his vision of the parallel development of the School and the Nation, he donated, not only the building, but also an impressive collection of American art, including distinguished works of Gilbert Stuart, Rembrandt Peale, Winslow Homer, Thomas Eakins, Paul Manship and Mary Cassatt. From Cochran's endowment fund other works were added, among them Bellows, Hassam, Hopper, Marin, Sloan, as well as comtemporary names, Calder, Lippold, Moholy-Nagy, Georgia O'Keeffe, Pollack, Shawn, and Phillips graduate Frank Stella. Inspired by Cochran's gift, the visual arts are exceptionally strong at the school these days and drama is flourishing.

The Armillary Sphere by the American sculptor Paul Manship stands on the lawn in front of the libary.

The skylight roof of the Addison Gallery.

The Mathematics Building is named for Samuel F.B. Morse, best known as the inventor of the telegraph and the "Morse" Code, who graduated in 1865. The Dupont family contributed generously to this building.

Overleaf: Rabbit Pond and the adjoining Moncrieff Cochran Sanctuary were part of a 125 acre gift by Thomas Cochran in memory of his brother, to provide a greater sense of nature and repose on the campus. Several dormitories face on the pond and it is a favorite spot for solitude and contemplation.

Bancroft Hall centers the residential "West Quad" and is named for Cecil F.P. Bancroft, the seventh headmaster, a pivotal figure in the life of Phillips Academy.

Bancroft, a graduate of Dartmouth and the Andover Theological Seminary, took office in 1873. For the nearly 100 previous years of its existence, the school had been dominated by the dogmatic Calvinism of Eliphalet Pearson's teaching. Among the consequences of this tradition was an alienation from Harvard, which had largely abandoned a religious affiliation, and Exeter, similarly unemcumbered. Although deeply religious himself, Bancroft emphasized the concept of Christian love, rather than discipline. After an extended visit to England's famous schools, Eton, Harrow, and Winchester, Bancroft broadened the courses of study and recruited a new, more liberal faculty, so distinguished that many left to head other schools, notably Edward Coy and David Comstock who founded Hotchkiss in 1893.

Whereas previously, contact with other schools had seemed to carry the risk of contamination with heretical ideas, Bancroft opened new relationships, particularly in athletics. The only prior recorded event was a baseball game with Tufts in 1866. Harvard, Yale and Dartmouth teams appeared occasionally, the Harvard relationship being the oldest continuous competition (1875), and the Exeter contests began in 1878.

By the end of his career, Bancroft had shaped the school for its role in the twentieth century. His successor, Alfred Stearns, grandson of the President of Amherst, completed the acquisition of the Andover Theological Seminary (Henry L. Stimson negotiated a facesaving arrangement whereby the theological faculty was merged into the Harvard Divinity School while Phillips acquired its facilities) and oversaw the physical restructuring accomplished by Thomas Cochran in the late 1920's and early 1930's.

Nathan Hale dormitory faces on Rabbit Pond.

Boarding students today account for about 1,000 of the 1,200 students in Phillips Acadamy (the remainder being day students living in the town of Andover) and are divided into five residential clusters. The total enrollment is about 60% boys and 40% girls and these proportions are maintained in each cluster, although boys and girls live in separate buildings within each cluster. Social life is not confined to the residential cluster and the spirit is free and open. The 1920's rule book, *Customs and Points for New Men*, put it this way, "always speak to an Andover man on the street, whether you know him or not." It also advised, "try to keep enlarging the number of your acquaintances, but be slow to make intimate friends."

A drama class in springtime.

Although no longer a requirement, as in the early years, religion remains a guiding influence in the school.

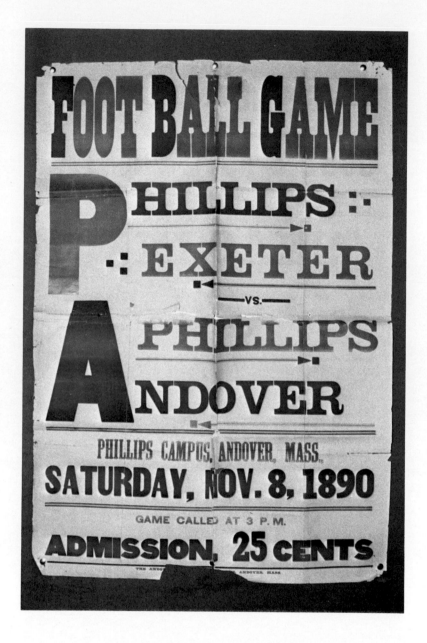

The captains meet for the coin flip.

The past . . .

. . . the future

Massed bands entertain at halftime.

Soccer is now the most popular sport for both boys and girls.

Andover has turned out many outstanding swimmers, the most famous being Jimmy McLane who won the Olympic 1500 meters at London in 1948 in the summer before his senior year. After a brilliant career at Yale, he repeated as a gold medal winner in the 1952 Olympics in Helsinki.

Hockey has long been a major sport and many Phillips graduates have distinguished themselves at the college level. Among Olympic team members are Jack Morrison of Yale; Ted Thorndike and Dan Bolduc from Harvard and John McBride from Princeton.

Winter: Samuel Phillips.

Spring: Borden Gym.

Back from the interscholastic crew championships.

Opposite: The girl's crew at the Head-of-the-Charles Regatta at Harvard, the highlight of the fall rowing season.

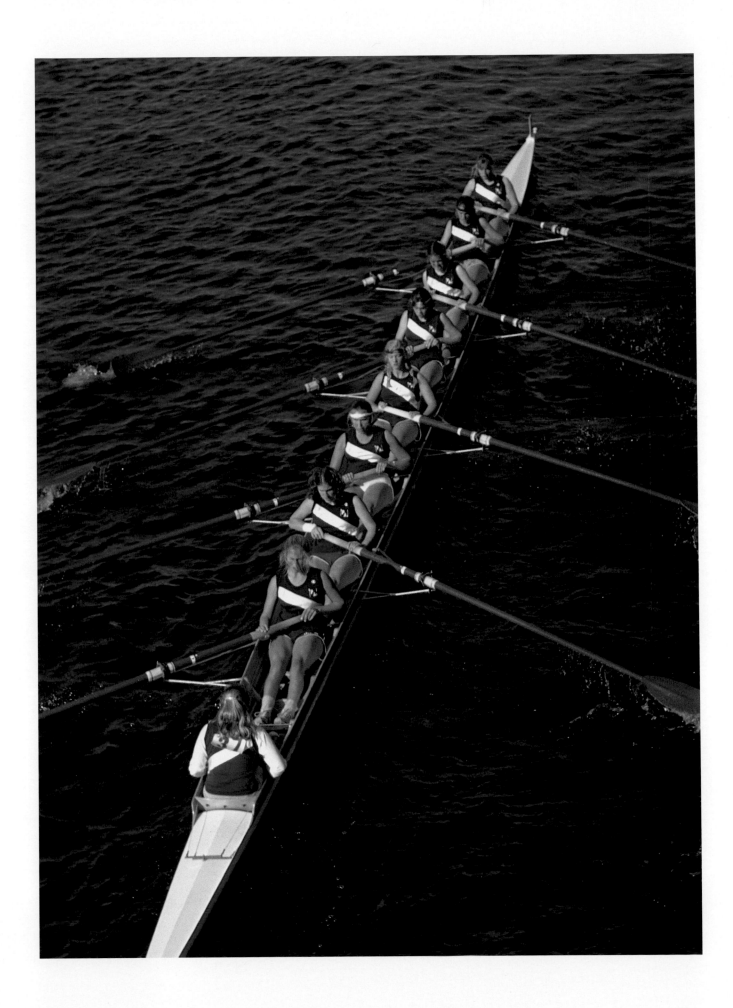

Stroke!

The athletic rivalry with Harvard is the oldest continuous competition, even predating Exeter. Harvard usually fields a combined freshman-J.V. team, as here.

Abbot Academy began in 1829 as the first Massachusetts school for women. It was merged into Phillips Academy in 1973.

At the time of its formation, one half of the women in New England were functionally illiterate. Few attended grammar school. The question: "Do females possess minds as capable of improvement as males?" was formally and seriously debated at Phillips Academy (and elsewhere) in 1827.

For those of us today who enjoy a co-educational atmosphere, it seems odd to contemplate that Mrs. Sara Abbot, a cousin of Samuel Phillips, pledged the first funds to the formation of the school on condition that it be located on School Street, not on Main Street, to avoid the temptations which might be present if the girls were present on the same street frequented by Phillips' boys. As late as 1900 a Phillips boy and an Abbot girl were "dismissed" from school for having been seen horseback riding together in Lawrence.

Abbot Hall, the first major building of Abbot Academy is considered the work of Charles Bulfinch.

A panel on the north face of Abbot Hall.

The roof of Graham House.

The bookstore is a frequent stop and a friendly fireplace and chairs are welcome on winter days.

Spring fever.

The Andover Inn was financed by Thomas Cochran and several friends, including his Morgan partner, Dwight Morrow, father-in-law of Charles Lindbergh.

Commons contains five handsome, paneled dining rooms. Work duties are shared equally by students.

Rabbit Pond reflections.

The Bagpipers lead the graduating class procession with the unforgettable "Scotland the Brave."

Headmaster Donald McNemar addresses the graduating class collectively on the steps of Sam Phil. . .

. . .and individually at a reception at his home.

Graduation audience.

The graduating class by tradition forms a great circle and diplomas are handed round until they reach the proper recipient.

Acknowledgements

I want to thank especially Tom Wyman for his graceful Foreword. His continuing interest and dedication to Phillips Academy, like that of many others over the years, no matter the demands of their careers and achievements, are part of the spirit which has carried the school through its history — and makes it what it is today.

The photographs in this book were taken during the academic years 1981-82 and 1982-83. From the first "hello" from Josh Minor, head of Admissions, to the last farewell from the headmaster, Don McNemar, at graduation, my years at Andover were full of friendships and thoughtful, helpful people. All of them, in one way or another, in feeling, if not in presence, contributed to this book. They are too numerous to name, but all are due my gratitude.

For factual material in the text, I have relied principally upon the detailed history of Phillips Academy, *Youth From Every Quarter*, by Fredrick S. Allis, Jr. published by the school on its Bicentennial in 1978; and the companion history of Abbot, *A Singular School*, by Susan McIntosh Lloyd, published by the school in 1979.

Also of interest are *The Andovers: Portrait of Two New England Towns* by Thea Wheelwright, with black and white photographs by Katharine Knowles; TBW Books, Woolwich, Maine; and *Exeter Impressions* by Robert Gambee, a study of the town of Exeter and the Phillips Exeter Academy, with black and white photographs, Hastings House, N.Y.

For a general background in the Pre-Revolutionary period, especially social and educational attitudes, I referred to Samuel Eliot Morison's *Oxford History of the American People*.

For those with a technical interest, I used Nikon cameras and the following Nikon lens: 28mm, 50 mm; and 35-105 mm and 80-200 mm zooms. During the spring of 1983 I also used a Hasselblad for certain shots. Dick and George Chapell of the Andover Photo Shop kept me supplied with film, mostly Ektachrome 64. The images in this book were selected from over 3,000 slides.

Lastly, my father, Charles Kelly, deserves special mention. His inspiration and encouragement brought the book into being; and his editing and criticism gave it final form. He also took several photographs during graduation weekend (while I was otherwise engaged) and he used his position as editor to insist that they be included.

Thanks, Dad, for everything.

Mia Kelly
Wayzata, Minnesota
July 1983